Focus

The focus of this book is:

- to provide a forum for discussion,
- to discriminate, giving reasons for choices.

Tuning In

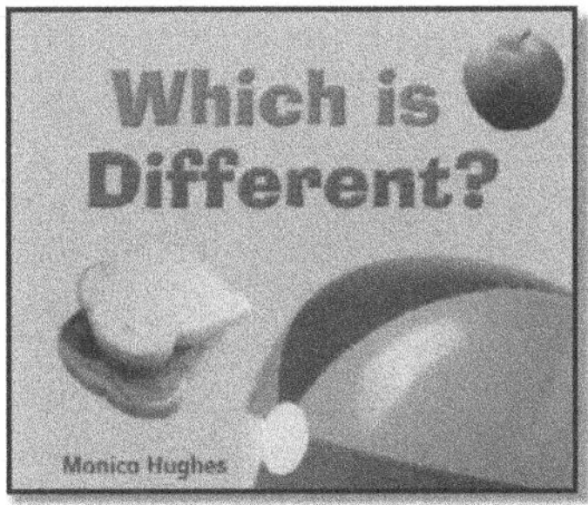

The front cover

We are going to read the title together and point to each word as we read it.

Did you notice the question mark at the end?

Speaking and Listening

Can you name the objects on the cover?

Can you tell us something about each one? Which one do you think is different? Why?

The back cover

Now let's read the back cover blurb.

Let's see if we can find the things that are different in the book.

Title page

Can you name the objects here?

Can you tell us something about each one?

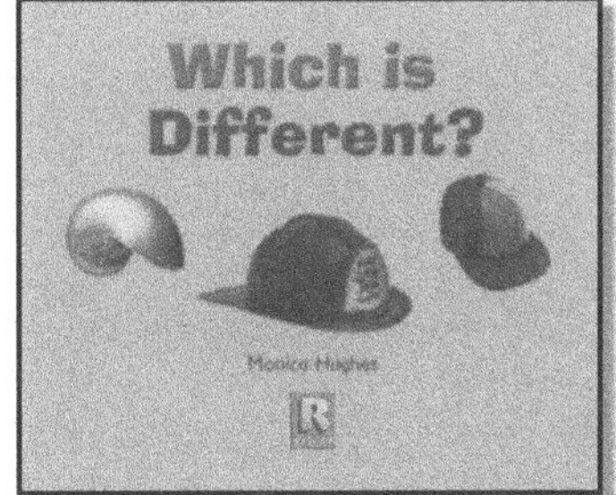

1

 **Tuning In**

Can you name the things here?

Tell us something about each of them.

Speaking and Listening

Which is different here? In what way is it different?

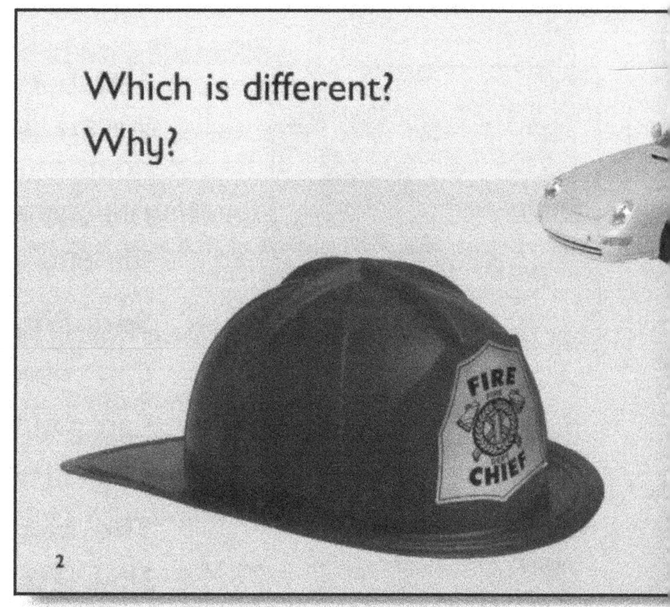

 **Observe and Prompt**

Word Recognition

- If the children have difficulty with the word 'Which', ask them if they recognise the initial letters and sound – 'wh', then model the reading of this word for them.

2

 **Observe and Prompt**

Language Comprehension

- Ask the children which item they think is different.

- Why do the children think this item is different?

- Check the reasons the children give for their choice. Point out there is more that one correct 'answer'.

 **Tuning In**

On these two pages there is a set of clothes and a set of things with stripes.

Speaking and Listening

Which one do you think is different? Why did you choose that one?

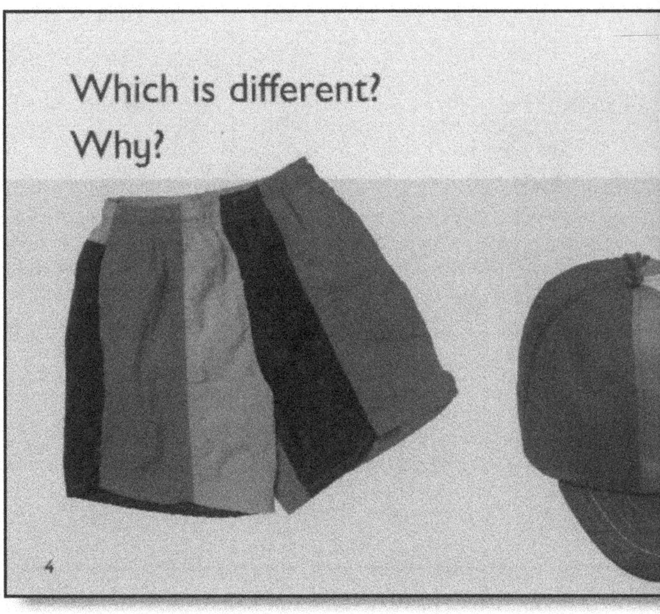

 **Observe and Prompt**

Word Recognition

- Check the children can read the sight word 'is'.

4

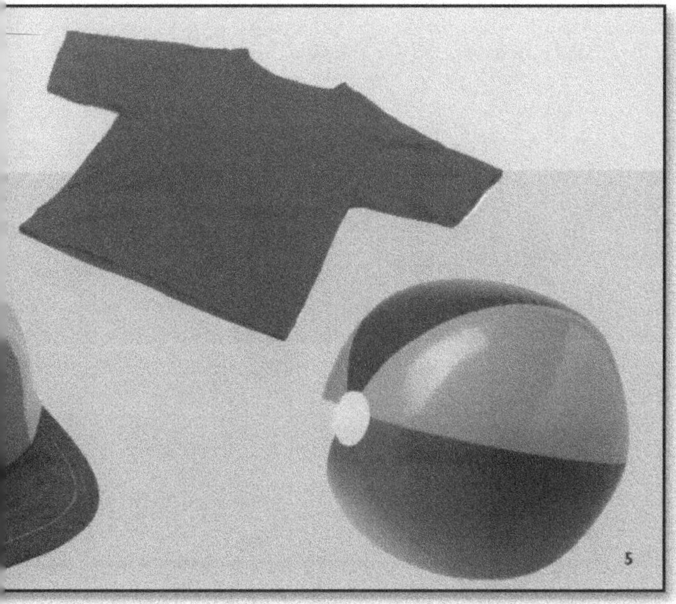

Observe and Prompt

Language Comprehension

- Ask the children which is different here. Why?
- Check the children understand that the important point is the reason for their choice.

 **Tuning In**

On these two pages there is a set of black and white animals.

Can you see any other sets?

Speaking and Listening

Which is different here?

 **Observe and Prompt**

Word Recognition

- If the children have difficulty with the word 'different', ask them if they recognise the initial letter and sound – 'd'. Then model the blending of this word for them.

 ## Observe and Prompt

Language Comprehension

- Which do the children think is different here?
- Ask the children to give a reason for their answer. What else might be different?

Tuning In

On these two pages there is a set of three farm animals.

Speaking and Listening

Which is different here?

Observe and Prompt

Word Recognition

- If the children have difficulty reading 'Why', model the reading of this word for them.

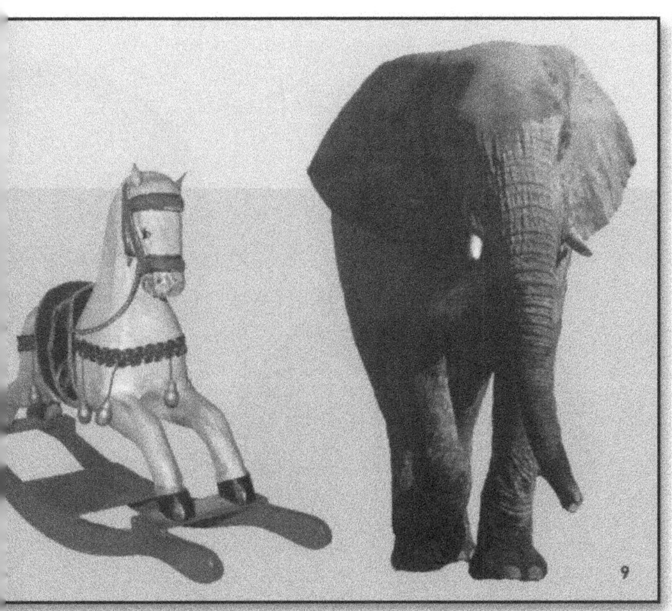

👁 Observe and Prompt

Language Comprehension

- Ask the children which is different on these pages.

- Ask the children to explain their choice.

- Does anyone in the class think something else is different? Why?

 **Tuning In**

On these two pages there is a set of smooth things.

Can you see any other sets?

Speaking and Listening

Which is different here? In what way is it different?

 **Observe and Prompt**

Word Recognition

● Check the children are reading the words with
more confidence.

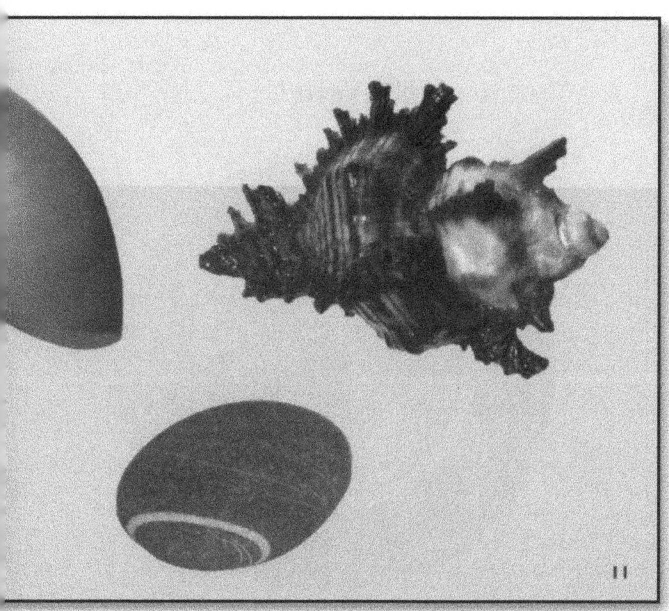

Observe and Prompt

Language Comprehension

- Observe the children read with appropriate phrasing and read the text as a question.

- Ask the children what these object are.

- Have the children ever seen any shells? Where?

- Which one do the children think is different? Why?

Tuning In

What sets can you see on these two pages?

Speaking and Listening

Which is different here? In what way is
it different?

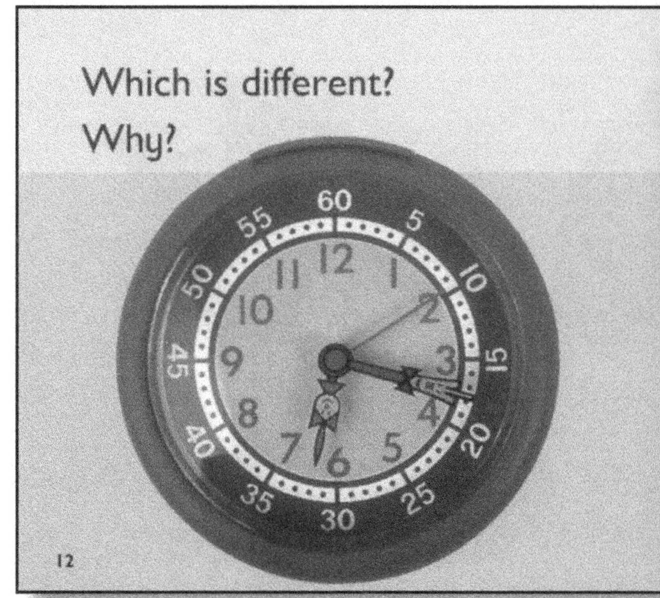

 **Observe and Prompt**

Word Recognition

- Check the children are beginning to use their decoding
  skills to read 'different'.

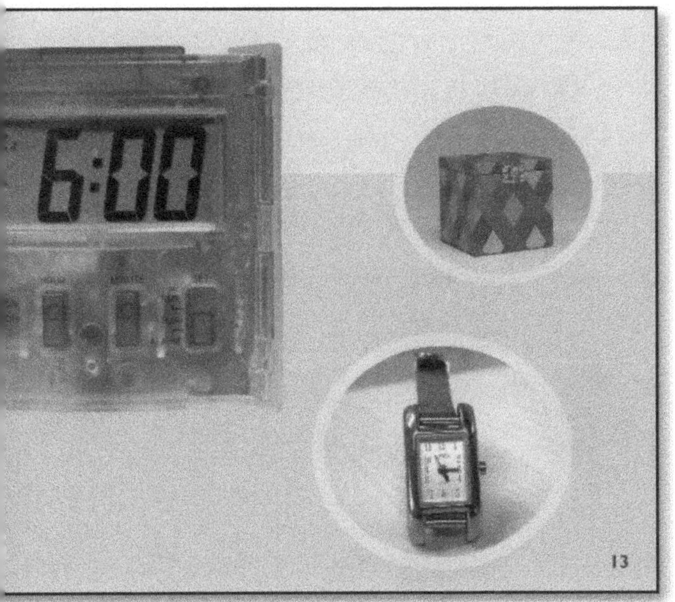

 **Observe and Prompt**

Language Comprehension

- Ask the children what objects there are here.
- Ask the children which sets they can see.

Tuning In

Can you name the things on these two pages?

Tell us something about each of them.

Speaking and Listening

What sets can you see on this page?

 **Observe and Prompt**

Word Recognition

- Check the children are more confident reading 'Which' and 'Why'.

Observe and Prompt

Language Comprehension

- Ask the children to name all the items they can see here.

- Which do the children think is different? Why?

- Does anyone else in the class think something else is different?

Tuning In

- This page has a list of all the things that are different – the odd ones out.

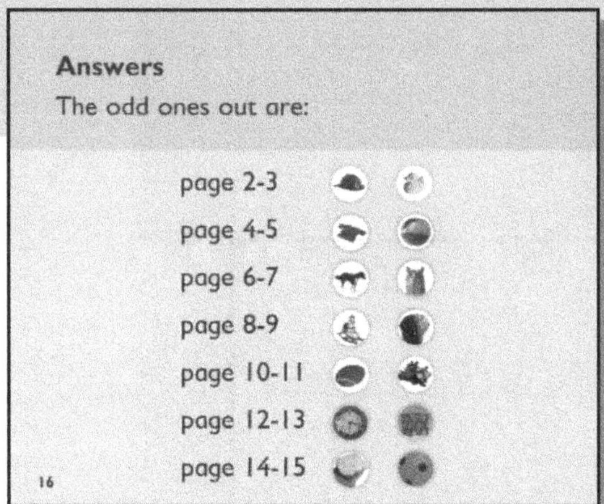

Observe and Prompt

Word Recognition

- The words 'Answers' and 'ones' will not be fully decodable for the children at this stage. Tell them these words.

- Check the children can read the sight words 'The', 'out' and 'are'.

- Check the children are using their decoding skills to read 'odd'. If they have difficulty, tell them that the double 'd' represents a single sound.

Language Comprehension

- Check the children understand the purpose of this 'Answers' page.

- Do the children understand how the circles show the odd ones out?

- Ask the children to look at pages 10 and 11. Are these the same things that were talked about?

The front cover

Does Korka look mighty?

How do you know he's an elf?

Where do you think is the place in the background?

It's where Korka lives – a place called 'Elf Hill'.

The back cover

Let's read the blurb.

How could a small elf like Korka stop the big trolls?

The title page

What is Korka doing in this picture? (*Sitting on a rock, thinking or daydreaming*)

What sort of character do you think he is?

This is the author and this is the illustrator.

This is the publisher's logo.

1

Read pages 2 and 3

READ

Purpose: To find out how the other elves treated Korka.

Pause at page 3

EXPLORE

What was Korka's problem? Were the other elves kind to him?

Read the words that the big elf said to him.

Tricky word (page 2):
The word 'elves' may be beyond the children's word recognition skills. Tell this word to the children.

2